DOG TALES

True Stories
of Heroic Hounds

written by Penelope Rich
illustrated by Isabel Muñoz

ARCTURUS

ARCTURUS

This edition published in 2022 by Arcturus Publishing Limited
26/27 Bickels Yard, 151–153 Bermondsey Street,
London SE1 3HA

Copyright © Arcturus Holdings Limited

Author: Penelope Rich
Illustrator: Isabel Muñoz
Editors: Stephanie Carey and Donna Gregory
Designer: Allie Oldfield
Art Direction: Rosie Bellwood
Editorial Manager: Joe Harris

ISBN: 978-1-83940-612-6
CH007774NT
Supplier 29, Date 1221, Print run 12059

Printed in China

CONTENTS

Our Relationship with Dogs

Dogs are often referred to as man's best friend, but of course they are everyone's best friend—man, woman, and child. They are very popular pets the world over, but they also do hundreds of useful jobs, from herding sheep to saving lives.

All dogs—as we know them today—are thought to have originated from wolves, thousands of years ago. If you look at a husky or a German Shepherd, you can see the similarity, but what about a tiny Chihuahua or Dachshund?

The reasons why today's dogs come in all shapes, sizes, and patterns is that people meddled with nature. They bred dogs with characteristics that were useful to them—traits including strength, intelligence, speed, or good hunting instincts.

People in snowy lands needed dogs that were strong enough to pull sledges and logs and that had thick coats that could cope with the cold. Others needed fast hunters to help catch food. For catching rabbits, people needed small dogs, who could follow the rabbits into small spaces. For hunting birds, people needed retrievers who would find the birds and bring them back.

Today, there are over 300 breeds of dog, all with their own characteristics. Many dogs still do the jobs they were bred for. Collies and koolies still round up livestock. Retrievers, spaniels, and water dogs still help hunters. But as the world has changed, so has the work that some breeds do. Greyhounds still chase rabbits, but the rabbits are not real, and the purpose is for sport, not hunting. Belgian Malinois were bred for herding, but now they are the most popular breed used by police forces and the military.

Many more dogs are now simply our pets. How we choose a pet dog is still sometimes down to breed—it might have the characteristics or look we like. Sometimes it's down to personality—whether we want a playful dog, for example, or a gentle dog. Sometimes we adopt an unwanted or badly treated dog, and sometimes a dog chooses us. However a dog comes into a home, they soon become part of the family.

It's proven that when an owner and their dog look at one another, a feel-good hormone is released in both the person and the dog. It's the same when we stroke them, or play with them. It is a mutual feeling, and it is called love.

Incredible Journeys

True stories about dogs and their incredible journeys are so universally popular that the news spreads fast. The stories are told and retold in newspapers, on the internet, in books, and in movies.

We marvel at dogs' survival instincts—how they can use their senses, intelligence, and wits to make it home or to help people get where they want to go. We are fascinated by incredible stories like that of Bobbie the Wonder Dog, who journeyed half way across America to get home. Without a map, a vehicle, or the ability to communicate with humans, just how did he do it? No one knows, but his story is not unique. There are many others around the world that show how devoted and loyal some dogs are to their owners.

And then there are the accidental tourists, the ones who find themselves going on extraordinary journeys without realizing it, such as Belka and Strelka who went into space, and Bothie who went on a round-the-world expedition and found himself at both the North and South Poles. It is gratifying to see how these dogs and others take such extraordinary journeys in their stride.

Explorers have taken dogs with them throughout history, both for their abilities and their companionship. Knowing their dogs would hear and smell danger well before them no doubt helped those explorers sleep better at night. But as well as keeping them safe, dogs would also keep them warm.

However, the most heartwarming stories are those about stray dogs who adopt a human being and decide they are going to go home with them. There are so many stories, like those of Antis, Gobi, and Arthur—dogs who had probably experienced the worst of human nature, but who still hoped to find that special someone who would love them and care for them. Dogs are remarkable, and we probably only know the half of what they are capable of.

Belka & Strelka

Belka and Strelka were two small stray dogs who had the most extraordinary adventure. They went into space for a day, along with 42 mice, a rabbit, two rats, a few fruit flies and some plants. They had been plucked from the streets of Moscow by the Russian space agency for the Vostok space program. The plan was to send a group of animals into space to see if they could survive the journey. If they did, it would give them confidence to launch the first person into space.

The scientists chose stray dogs because they were hardier and would be more able to cope with the stresses of the training and flight. They chose females because they are calmer and smaller. Belka, which means "Squirrel" in Russian, and Strelka, which means "Arrow", had to pass a number of tests before they became fully qualified astro-dogs. They were put on vibrating beds to get used to the movement, and spun around in a machine called a centrifuge (like a super-fast fairground ride) to get used to the G-forces. They passed all the tests.

When the launch day came, in August 1960, the dogs were put into the capsule and placed in the tip of the rocket. The launch was successful, and they orbited the Earth 18 times. The return to Earth is the most dangerous time, so everyone held their breath, but the capsule parachuted gently to the ground. Belka and Strelka were national heroes. Everyone wanted to see them, and there was a big press conference with the world watching. The following year, a cosmonaut called Yuri Gagarin made the same journey, orbiting Earth once before returning safely. Belka and Strelka had paved the way.

The two dogs went on to live long, happy lives. Strelka had puppies, one of which was given to the then US President's wife, Jackie Kennedy.

Antis

Early in World War II, Czech airman Robert Bozdech and his pilot were on a mission over northern France when their plane was shot down. The pilot was injured, so Robert ran to a farmhouse to find help. All he found was a little German Shepherd puppy, abandoned and hungry. Robert tucked the puppy inside his jacket. They would be companions for life, and they went through many near-death experiences together.

Robert and the other Czech airmen had to escape France quickly when the German forces arrived. They tried to make it to North Africa, but their ship was torpedoed, and Robert and Antis nearly drowned. They were rescued, and were taken back to Britain, where Robert spent the next five years in the Royal Air Force. One evening, Robert and Antis were caught in a bombing raid. Antis was not a trained search-and-rescue dog, but he found six people and a baby buried under the rubble. He returned back to base a hero.

Robert flew many missions for the RAF, and Antis would always wait for his return by the runway. He knew before anyone else when the planes were returning, and would stand up in anticipation. When Robert's plane did not return one day, Antis spent two days looking at the sky. Robert's plane had come under attack and he had been injured. The men looked after Antis, but he wouldn't move and hardly ate until Robert returned. When he was better, Robert resumed his flying duties. Antis wasn't going to let Robert leave him again, so he boarded the plane unnoticed. Robert discovered him mid-flight. After that, Antis flew on many more missions, until he was badly injured by a piece of flying metal.

After the war, they had a few years of peace back in Czechoslovakia, before Robert had to flee again. The escape was dangerous, but Antis led him and others to safety. They ended up back in Britain, and Antis lived to the grand old age of 14.

SOUTH AUSTRALIA

STOP ME NOT BUT FOR I AM BOB THE DRIVER'S DOG LET ME JOG

Bob

Bob was a scruffy Collie who lived a free-roaming life on the South Australia railroad in the 1880s. He was such a familiar face on the trains that a passenger had a special collar made for him with a plate that said, "Stop me not but let me jog, for I am Bob the driver's dog."

When he was a puppy, Bob lived with a man who ran a hotel near Adelaide. The railway was being built nearby and Bob became fascinated with it, spending more time there than at home. One day, a rabbiter took Bob and a number of other strays to become rabbit hunters. Rabbits were real pests in Australia at that time, destroying wildlife and crops. Farmers and landowners would employ rabbiters, and their dogs would catch the rabbits.

On the train north, the guard, William Ferry, took a liking to Bob and offered to buy him. The rabbiter said that he would trade Bob for another stray. William found another stray to trade, and Bob became his companion on the railway network. William later took a station master's job, but Bob didn't want to be confined to a station. He remained a free spirit and his journeys took him thousands of miles across Southern Australia, choosing which trains to travel on. He was friends with all the enginemen, who always let Bob jump on board. At night, Bob would follow them home in the hope of getting a meal, and would return with them the next day. He particularly liked sitting on top of the coal box, loving the big whistles and the belching smokestacks. He switched to riding on trams when he fancied it, and even jumped onto the odd paddle steamer downriver once in a while.

News of Bob the railway dog spread throughout Australia. It is said that he lived to a good age, and his collar is on display in the National Railway Museum in Port Adelaide. In 2009, a statue of Bob was unveiled in Peterborough, where Bob and William first met.

Bobbie

Bobbie was a handsome Scottish Collie dog, who became worldwide news when he made it back home after getting lost on a family trip 2,500 miles (4,000 km) away. No one knows how Bobbie made it home, but it is well documented how he was lost.

Bobbie was the beloved pet of the Brazier family, who owned the Reo Lunch Restaurant in Silverton, Oregon, USA. In February 1924, they packed up their car and went to visit family in Wolcott, Indiana, taking Bobbie with them. When they stopped to get fuel near Wolcott, some local dogs attacked Bobbie and chased him away. After days of searching, the Braziers accepted he was lost and returned home heartbroken. They thought someone would find him, and left instructions to send him back on the railroad, but they had no word of him for six months. One day, one of the Brazier daughters was walking along Main Street when she saw a dog walking toward her. He was thin and matted, his claws were worn and his paws were sore, but as he got closer, she knew it was Bobbie! She brought him back to the restaurant for a joyful reunion. Bobbie was treated to a feast of meat and ice cream.

How he had crossed six or seven states, and the Rocky Mountains in winter, is a mystery but the story of Bobbie the wonder dog was told all around the world. The Braziers started to receive letters from people who had looked after Bobbie on his journey, along with bags full of fan mail.

UNITED STATES

Bobbie played himself in a film called *The Call of the Wild*, and went on to father 15 puppies, all male. One of them, Pal, led Silverton's first pet parade—an event that is now held every year.

Explorer Dogs

Throughout history, dogs have accompanied intrepid explorers on their expeditions up mountains, and across continents and oceans.

Leoncico was the companion of Vasco Núñez de Balboa, a Spanish explorer who sailed to the Americas in the sixteenth century in search of riches. Leoncico was such a valued companion that Balboa took him as a stowaway, hidden in a barrel, to Panama. They trekked together from the east coast to the west, the first Europeans to see the Pacific Ocean. Leoncico was paid a soldier's wages and had a golden collar.

In 1768, botanist Sir Joseph Banks took his greyhound, Lady, on Captain Cook's first great voyage around the world, sailing west around the tip of South America into the then-uncharted waters of the South Pacific. As well as being a companion, Lady helped Banks to catch animals for him to study, as well as to eat.

In 1805, Seaman, a huge Newfoundland water dog, accompanied Americans Lewis and Clark on their two-year expedition to explore the largely unmapped area between the Mississippi River and the Pacific coast. Seaman proved to be a good hunter and a vigilant guard dog.

Later, in 1871, a beagle-cross called Tschingel was part of a team of three men and one woman who were the first to climb numerous peaks in the Swiss and French Alps. All the mountain guides in Chamonix celebrated Tschingel's historic ascent of the highest peak, Mont Blanc. Many other dogs, like Mera (page 27), have followed in her pawprints.

And there is one little dog who came before Belka and Strelka in the story of space exploration. Her name was Laika—another Russian stray. She was the first animal to orbit Earth, and she did it all alone. She was the first living being to see the whole Earth from space—a true pioneer.

SOUTH KOREA

Daejeon

Jindo

JAPAN

Baekgu

Baekgu's story is one of another incredible journey: 186 miles (300 km) from the South Korean mainland to Jindo Island off the south coast. Baekgu is a Jindo, a breed of white dog specific to the island, and they are renowned for their loyalty. In 1993, Baekgu proved just how loyal they can be.

Baekgu's owner was an 83-year-old lady, Park Bok-dan, who lived on Jindo Island and was too old and too tired to cope with Baekgu's large litters of puppies. Reluctantly, she sold Baekgu, who ended up living with a nice family in Daejeon, 186 miles (300 km) north of Jindo Island. Baekgu obviously missed home, because seven months later, there was scratching at Mrs. Park's door. When she went to investigate, Park Bok-dan was amazed to find Baekgu, thin and exhausted, on the doorstep. Somehow, Baekgu had known to head south. She found her way back to the coast, and crossed over the bridge that joins the island from the mainland. It's a mystery how she did it.

Mrs. Park took Baekgu back in and the dog was never far from her side from that day on. The story spread nationwide, and it was made all the more special because Jindos are so loved by the South Koreans that the breed is their 53rd National Treasure. Jindos even featured in the Olympic opening ceremony when it was held in the capital, Seoul, in 1988. A computer company picked up Baekgu's story and used it for a popular television advert, which made her famous. Following that, she became the subject of comics, a children's book, and even a musical.

Baekgu died seven years after her incredible journey, and there is now a statue dedicated to her and Mrs. Park on the island. It's a touching statue, capturing the moment in time when Mrs. Park greeted Baekgu on the morning of her return. It ensures their story will never be forgotten.

Balto & Togo

Balto and Togo were two Siberian huskies who, in 1925, led an extraordinary rescue mission—in unimaginable cold—across the icy Arctic to save the lives of up to 10,000 people.

Balto has been immortalized with his own statue in Central Park in New York, which is a little unfair to Togo and the other dogs who were also part of the team that journeyed more than 1,085 km (674 miles) to reach the town of Nome in Alaska.

In 1925, Nome was completely cut off by the harshest winter in 20 years, so an outbreak of diphtheria couldn't have come at a worse time. Diphtheria is a potentially fatal disease that affects the nose and throat. Untreated, it spreads quickly, but a vaccine was available. The problem facing Nome's Board of Health was that the Postal Service usually took 25 days to get there, but the vaccine would only last for six.

It was a race against time. Together the Postal Service and the Board of Health set up a relay of 20 dog-sled teams to make the journey from the end of the train line in Nenana to Nome. They called on renowned dog-sled driver Leonhard Seppala to take the toughest leg. Seppala had a brilliant team of dogs, led by the best of them all, Togo. They took delivery of the vaccine with just two days left to go, so Seppala made the decision to cross an unstable ice sheet in a blizzard in order to get the vaccine to Nome in time.

He could see nothing, so he had to rely on Togo's super-powers. Togo got them through safely, so they could hand over the vaccine to Charlie Olsen and his lead dog, Jack, who then met Gunnar Kaasen and Balto.

Racing the final 85 km (53 miles), Kaasen and Balto reached Nome in time to avert disaster. So Balto's statue is really for all those dogs who, over those six days, showed how brave, loyal, and immeasurably special dogs can be.

Togo
1913–1929

Balto
1919–1933

Bothie

Bothie was a fearless, funny Jack Russell Terrier who became the first dog to reach both the North and South Poles. He was given to the adventurers and polar explorers Ranulph and Virginia Fiennes as a puppy. They adored him, but what would they do with him while they were on a three-year expedition? They decided to take him with them.

The Transglobe Expedition was a journey around the world, from the UK to Antarctica, then up to the Arctic and back again. The Fiennes consulted a vet about taking Bothie. The vet said his fur would grow thicker in the cold, but they should be careful with his ears and feet, so they bought him a hood, some booties, and a coat in preparation. Bothie didn't travel all the way with his owners. He flew to South Africa and then sailed on a large research ship to Antarctica. On board, Bothie marked his territory by leaving smelly "presents" in everyone's cabins. As a result, not all the crew loved him, but most enjoyed his company.

When Bothie experienced the Antarctic ice for the first time, he yawned, licked his paws, and barked at the albatrosses and penguins. He also had a dangerous encounter with a southern skua—a huge bird with a vicious beak, who could have easily picked Bothie up and flown away with him.

Ranulph and two team members trekked over the ice to the South Pole, but Bothie arrived by plane on 15 December 1980. They famously had a cricket match there just before Christmas. Almost a year and a half later, they made it to the North Pole, and Bothie became famous as the dog who had been where no other dog had been before.

Arthur

Mikael Lindnord is an adventure racer, one of a team of three men and one woman that races for days, crossing mountains, rivers, and deserts by bike, kayak, or on foot. Adventure races are as tough as any race can get.

In 2014, Mikael was the leader of a Swedish team in the Adventure Racing World Championships in Ecuador, South America. The race was 700 km (436 miles) from mountain to sea, through the Amazonian rain forest. By the time they had got to the finish line, they were a team of five—three men, one woman, and a dog they named Arthur.

Mikael met Arthur on day four, in a transition area, where they and other racers were changing from a cycling stage to a trekking stage. In these transition areas, racers prepare for the next stage, sleep, and eat, to get the energy they need. Mikael was preparing a meal of meatballs and pasta in a thermal pack, when he noticed a dog watching him. Mikael had seen many dogs on the trip, but this one was different. There was a nasty wound on his back, so Mikael shared some meatballs with him. This one act of kindness was clearly all it took for the dog to adopt Mikael and the team as his new friends. He began to follow them, through mud and across rivers, and the team shared their rations with him. When they came to the kayaking stage, they were not allowed to take a dog, so with heavy hearts they left him on the river bank, but he dived in anyway, not wanting to be left behind. He wasn't a strong swimmer, so Mikael took the decision to take care of his new friend, Arthur, and dragged him into the boat. They didn't win the race, but it didn't matter.

Mikael took Arthur back to Sweden and wrote a book about their adventures. It starts, "Meeting Arthur and bringing him home is the single best thing I have ever done." The team now have a charity dedicated to helping street dogs in Ecuador.

Mera

In November 2018, Mera became the first dog to reach the summit of Baruntse, the highest point to which any dog has ever climbed—and she wasn't even part of an expedition. Baruntse is in the Himalayas, and is part of the same mountain range as Everest, the world's highest mountain. Mountaineers come from far and wide to climb these peaks, staying in camps up the mountain before attempting to reach the top. Don Wargowsky was leading a month-long expedition, taking a team of six people up Baruntse. The team stayed in the Nepalese town of Kare before their climb, where they met Mera for the first time. She paid them little attention then, but a few days later, after they had climbed the smaller Mera Peak, she suddenly came bounding up the mountain toward them, making a beeline for Wargowsky. They bonded immediately. Wargowsky named her Mera and let her sleep in his tent to keep them both warm.

When the local Sherpas went up the mountain to fix ropes to help the team climb, Mera went with them. These Nepalese men, who climbed these mountains regularly, had never seen anything like it. She was a natural climber. When the team started their climb to the next camp, Wargowsky tied Mera up so she would stay, but she chewed through the rope and caught up with them an hour later. He couldn't take her back, so she stayed with them.

They left that camp at 2am in the morning for the final climb to the top. Mera was asleep, and Wargowsky was pleased because she wouldn't follow them, but seven hours into the climb, Mera bounded toward them, unfazed by the steep drop-offs either side of the ridge, or the deep, cold snow. High altitude can make you very sick, so only one person was well enough to reach the summit with Wargowsky—and one dog. Mera was a phenomenon. Back at base-camp, the local expedition manager was so in awe of Mera that he offered to take her home. "She's special," he said, and he renamed her Baru, after the mountain she had conquered.

GOBI MARCH 2016

Gobi

In 2016, an Australian named Dion Leonard was a participant in an ultramarathon—a 250-km (155-mile) race across the Gobi Desert in China. On day two, he was joined by a little sandy-haired dog, who had been in camp the night before, scrounging food from the runners. At the start the next morning, the little dog was by Dion's feet, fascinated by the yellow gaiters wrapped around his running shoes to keep out the dust and stones. As he ran, she followed his feet, but as the race progressed, she started to run alongside him. Dion thought she would turn back at any minute, but she stayed with him as they crossed the Tien Shan, one of the largest mountain ranges in China. She snuggled up with him in his tent that night and ran with him for the next two days.

The racing on days four and five were brutal in searing heat, so Dion arranged for her to go with the race officials in their car, but she was with Dion when he crossed the finish line. By then, he had named her Gobi and had decided he was going to take her back to his home in Scotland.

That was a challenge even harder than the race itself. Dion left Gobi in the care of some Chinese friends in Urumqi, who had agreed to look after her until she could travel, but she ran out of an open door and disappeared.

Dion flew back to China to start the search, launching a poster and social media campaign. The whole city, it seemed, began to look for Gobi, but days went by and Dion was worried he'd never see her again. Then he got a call from a man who had found a little dog in a park. It was Gobi and they were happily reunited. She now lives with Dion and his wife in Edinburgh, Scotland, and he told their story in a bestselling book. As one of the other race competitors put it: "Any dog that tough deserves a happy ending."

Hero Dogs

Dogs are important to the police, the military, search-and-rescue teams, and conservationists all around the world. They use their amazing senses and abilities to guard, protect, find, and rescue. Dogs, such as guide dogs, assistance dogs, and therapy dogs are also invaluable to those with disabilities who need help to live independent lives.

Wonderful examples of these amazing dogs are Roselle and Trakr, heroes of the 9/11 attacks on the World Trade Center. Roselle was the guide dog of Michael Hingson who was working on the 78th floor when the planes hit. She could have run to save herself, but she calmly guided Michael and 30 others down a stairwell full of smoke to safety. Trakr was one of the many search-and-rescue dogs who worked to find those buried under the rubble. He located the last survivor, and then collapsed from smoke inhalation, burns, and exhaustion.

Some experts believe that dogs do heroic things because they are pack animals. A pack animal is socially bonded to the other pack members. It is in their nature to protect one another, and dogs see their owners and handlers as their leaders, and their families as their pack.

For most working dogs, being a hero is all in a day's work. They don't seek praise or reward. They are so well trained that they know what is expected of them. But sometimes, like Roselle and Trakr, these working dogs do something so astonishingly brave that they deserve a medal, and that's where the PDSA Dickin Medal and Gold Medal come in. These are the two highest awards an animal can receive.

The Dickin Medal was introduced in Britain in 1943 to recognize the bravery and devotion to duty of animals serving in World War II. It has been awarded to 71 animals to date, and 34 of them are dogs, including Roselle. The Gold Medal is for those civilian animals who show the same level of bravery and devotion. Many countries have awards to celebrate their own national canine heroes. Trakr was given an award for Extraordinary Service to Humanity.

Stubby

Stubby is one of the most famous canine heroes of World War I. He was a stray Bull Terrier puppy who was adopted by Private J. Robert Conroy at a training camp for soldiers. Conroy named him Stubby because of his tail, but he also had short little legs and a stubby nose, so the name suited him well.

Dogs were not allowed in Conroy's infantry regiment, but Stubby cheered up the soldiers who were preparing to go to war, so they let him stick around. He joined in with the drills and even learned how to salute, putting his paw up to his eye.

When the regiment set sail from the US to France, Conroy smuggled Stubby on board, tucked into his coat. When he was discovered by Conroy's commanding officer at sea, Stubby's salute was enough to turn him from a stowaway to the infantry mascot.

Stubby served on the front line with Conroy for eight months, and proved to be a valuable member of the regiment. He killed rats who would eat the regiment's food, warned them of incoming artillery shells long before the soldiers could hear them, and alerted them to gas attacks long before the soldiers could smell the gas. Stubby had his own gas mask, and when his regiment took back a French town, some ladies made him a little coat on which the soldiers pinned medals. He proved to be excellent at finding wounded soldiers and would comfort them before the medics arrived. He also captured a German spy one night by biting him on the leg and keeping him in one place until help arrived.

By the end of the war, Stubby had served in 17 battles, and was wounded twice. In recognition of all this, he was made a sergeant and a new gold medal was attached to his coat.

On Stubby's return to the United States, he took part in many parades, and met three presidents.

Chips

When the United States entered World War II in 1942, the army asked people to donate their dogs to be trained for guard and patrol duty. The Wren family from New York sent their dog Chips, who was only two years old. He was a big dog, part German Shepherd, part Collie, and part Husky. He had bitten the garbage collectors, so the Wrens thought he would make a good guard dog. They were right. Chips became a hero, serving for three years on active duty in Italy, France, and North Africa.

Chips' real moment of glory came in 1943, when an enemy machine-gun crew had US forces pinned down on a beach on the Italian island of Sicily. Chips broke free from his handler and jumped into the gunner's nest. After the gunfire, a soldier appeared with Chips at his throat, and at that point the rest of the machine-gun crew surrendered. Chips was injured but still helped to find ten more enemy soldiers that day.

More than 11,000 dogs served with the US Army and Marine Corps in World War II, but Chips was awarded the most medals, and was nominated for a Purple Heart for the wounds he received in Italy. He met Presidents Roosevelt and Eisenhower, who went to pet Chips not realizing he had been trained to bite anyone he didn't know!

Chips was sent home to the Wren family in a crate in 1945. His medals were taken away when people objected to animals being given awards over soldiers, but that didn't really matter. The Wrens were just glad to have their pet home. The medals were later reinstated, but Chips was the last dog to receive military medals. Chips was recommended for the PDSA Dickin Medal in 2018. John Wren, who was only four years old when Chips went off to war, attended the ceremony, alongside Ayron, a serving dog who accepted the medal on Chips' behalf, in a show of respect from one military dog to another.

War Dogs

Dogs have been going to war with soldiers for centuries. They were sent into battle with spiked collars and metal coats for protection to fight for their masters. But in World War I, dogs took on many different roles. They became guard dogs, sentries, message carriers, cable layers, search-and-rescue dogs, and pack animals.

The Belgian army used large dogs to pull their machine guns to the front line. The German army used them to detect gas, issuing the dogs with special gas masks so they weren't harmed. Just like Sergeant Stubby (page 33), dogs were also excellent at finding wounded soldiers. They would carry medical supplies and stay with the injured soldiers until help arrived. But one of the most important roles that dogs had was as mascots, boosting morale and offering companionship and affection.

On the outbreak of World War II, countries around the world began to enlist animals into the war effort. Families gave up their beloved dogs, like Chips (page 35), hoping they would be useful, and many proved to be far more than that.

Another famous dog from World War II was a little Yorkshire Terrier called Smoky. She was a pocket-sized dog, found in New Guinea in the South Pacific, who went wherever Corporal William Wynne went. Her most notable achievement was when she helped to run a telegraph cable through a long, very narrow pipe.

The Russians had dogs to help them with wounded soldiers. One team of Samoyed sled dogs carried 1,239 soldiers away from the battlefield.

In Britain, search-and-rescue dogs were invaluable when bombs started to rain down on cities and towns, destroying buildings. Beauty was one of the first. She was a Wirehaired Terrier, and her special skill was locating animals trapped under rubble. She rescued 63 animals, as well as people.

More recently, more than 5,000 American dogs served in the Vietnam War in the 1960s, and many dogs were trained to detect mines in the Iraq invasion in 2003. It is sad to put dogs in such stressful and dangerous situations, but their contribution helps to save lives and lift spirits.

Bamse

Bamse is one of the many canine heroes of World War II. The St. Bernard dog from Honningsvåg in Norway arrived in the Scottish port of Montrose on board the Norweigan minesweeper *Thorodd*.

Bamse means "teddy bear" in Norwegian, and he was just that—a huge bundle of soft fur with a gentle spirit. He was the pet of the Hafto family, and when Captain Erling Hafto went to war, Bamse went with him. Wearing his protective steel helmet, Bamse would stand guard on deck until danger had passed.

When docked in Montrose, Bamse had his own bus pass, which hung around his neck, and bus drivers would let him on board. He would round up the ship's crew, and if any of them got into trouble with the locals, he stood up on his hind legs to protect them. He was as tall as a man, wider and stronger, with a mouthful of teeth. Bamse was not a dog to mess with.

Everyone who met Bamse, loved him. He would play soccer with the sailors on deck, and the locals would come to watch. Afterward, he would give the children rides on his back.

In 1941, a man tried to attack crew member Lt. Commander Olav Nilsen on the dockside in Dundee. Bamse knocked the attacker into the water. And in 1942, he rescued a sailor who had fallen overboard but couldn't swim. Despite barking, no immediate help came, so Bamse dived in, allowing the drowning sailor to grab hold of him before help finally arrived.

When Bamse died, he was buried in a full ceremony in Montrose, with a coffin draped in a Norwegian flag.

In 2006, Bamse was awarded the PDSA Gold Medal for "saving the lives of two members of the crew and his unstinting devotion to duty."

Hairy Man

In 1828, the sailing ship Despatch left Ireland, heading for Canada, carrying around 200 Irish immigrants and 11 crew. As the ship approached the coast of Newfoundland, during a heavy storm, it hit a rock. It must have been terrifying for the people on board, who were forced into the stormy waters.

Two days later, fisherman George Harvey found some wreckage along the beach and knew there had been a shipwreck. When the storm had died down enough, he went out in his small boat with his 17-year-old daughter, Ann, his 12-year-old son, Sam, and their Newfoundland dog, Hairy Man, to look for survivors. They found a small group of exhausted survivors on a beach, and rowed out to find more. They found a large group on a rocky island three miles out, but they couldn't get close enough to rescue them without damaging their own boat. There was only one thing for it: Hairy Man would swim to the island to create a rope line for the people to hang on to while they swam to the boat. Newfoundland dogs are naturally good swimmers. They have waterproof fur, webbed toes, and they are big, strong, and incredibly powerful. George Harvey knew that Hairy Man would get to the island easily—his dog wasn't in danger.

Over the next couple of days, the Harveys and Hairy Man saved around 160 people in this way. It was an extraordinary rescue story. Back at home, the Harveys shared all their food with the survivors and helped to erect makeshift shelters for them. Help didn't arrive for another few days, but when it did, their food was restored and the Harveys received a medal and a handwritten note from British King George IV. They also received £100, which was a large sum of money in those days. It's not clear if Hairy Man's contribution to the rescue was recognized at the time, but we now know what a true hero he was.

Morocho

Morocho is a Dogo Argentino, a type of dog that is bred in Argentina to be a strong, muscular hunting dog, protective of humans. The breed was developed by Dr. Antonio Nores Martinez in the 1920s. He crossed various breeds, including the Great Dane, the English Bull Terrier, the Boxer, and the Mastiff, to get a dog that had all the characteristics he wanted in a hunting dog—power, loyalty, courage, and strong hunting instincts. Morocho lives on the farm of Dr. Martinez's grandson, who continues to breed Dogo Argentinos.

In 2008, Morocho proved himself to be the perfect example of the family's careful breeding, when he saved the lives of two young members of his family from a puma. Also known as a cougar or mountain lion, the puma is one of the largest predators in South America. The girls had run down to pick figs from a tree on the farm. When they started to climb the tree to get the best figs on the higher branches, they were shocked to see a puma hiding in the branches above them. They were very scared, so they ran, but the puma ran after them. Luckily the girls had Morocho with them. Morocho stood his ground and confronted the puma, while the girls ran screaming back to the farmhouse. Their father heard their screams and came running. What he found was a badly injured Morocho and a dead puma. It must have been a fierce fight between the dog and the wild cat—a fight for their lives.

A family member carried Morocho back to the farmhouse. He was badly mauled and bitten, but over the next couple of weeks they slowly nursed him back to health. Brave doesn't even begin to describe Morocho. He makes the family feel safe when he's around. For the girls he is their protector, and their hero.

Czarue

The story of Czarue proves that even little stray dogs can be heroes. He probably saved the life of Julia, a three-year-old girl who had wandered away from home in the night.

When Julia stayed with her grandmother in Pierzwin in Poland, she played with Czarue, a little black Terrier crossbreed. Czarue was a village dog—he belonged to no one, and got food wherever he could. Julia asked her grandmother to bring him in and give him bread, but he was a free spirit, not a pet, and he lived his life on the streets.

One evening in 2013, Julia's grandmother went to check on Julia, but she wasn't asleep in her bed. Alarmed, she called in the emergency services and, along with more than 100 villagers, they spent the night searching for her in the forest surrounding the village in sub-zero temperatures. They even had a helicopter searching from above. They eventually found Julia the following morning when they heard a dog barking, and then Julia's cry. She was crying for her mother. She had walked four miles away from the village and was lying on the ground with Czarue by her side. She was wet and had mild frostbite, but luckily Czarue had kept her warm through the night.

Fire officer Szymonowski said: "For the whole night the animal was with the girl, it never left her. Remember, it was freezing and the child was wet." He acknowledged that Czarue was the most important factor in Julia's survival. The newspapers reported that they took Julia to the hospital to treat her hands and feet, but they didn't say what happened to Czarue. Let's hope the villagers gave him a nice warm meal and the appreciation he deserved for being such a good friend.

Ajax

In 2013, a gorgeous, bushy-coated German Shepherd called Ajax became the first Spanish dog to receive the PDSA Gold Medal, the non-military equivalent of the Dickin Medal. It is given to animals who display outstanding bravery and dedication, and in 2009, Ajax did just that when he saved many lives by detecting a hidden bomb.

Ajax is now the most famous of Spain's kennel of Civil Guard police dogs—highly trained animals who use their superior sense of smell to detect explosives. In July 2009, Ajax and his handler, Sergeant Juan Carlos Alabarces Muñoz, were part of team asked to search an area in Palma Nova on the island of Majorca. Hours before, a terrorist bomb had killed two officers, and the police suspected there was another bomb. Ajax set to work and found it hidden underneath a car in a popular tourist spot. Had it exploded without warning, it could have killed many people, but the bomb squad cleared the area and safely detonated the bomb, so no one was hurt.

Sergeant Muñoz said, "Ajax and I have worked together for over nine years—we're partners, and this strong relationship means that even with one small look or signal from him, I know straight away that he is telling me something. It is wonderful to see his actions rewarded with the PDSA Gold Medal—there is no other medal quite like this which truly recognizes the role of animals in society."

Ajax was 12 years old and retired from the bomb squad when he received his medal. Afterward, Ajax and Sergeant Muñoz were invited to meet Spain's King Juan Carlos at his palace in Madrid. The King had been due on the island days after the terrorist attack, so he wanted to thank them personally for their heroic actions that day.

Graf

Graf is one of an elite squad of dogs, working for the French national police. He is a highly trained Belgian Malinois, a breed employed by police forces and military around the world. They have a superior sense of smell, a wide field of vision, and they are fast. They can run up to 50 km/h (30 mph), and their bite is stronger than a shark's! Only one dog in 40 gets through the selection process, which shows how exceptional Graf is. The training includes helicopters, abseiling, swimming, noise, and lots of stressful situations. The dogs must be brave, sociable, and happy to work in a team. Graf's particular skill is apprehending and biting criminals. Often, the criminals will have a weapon, so Graf is sent into a situation before his handler, Lionel, and the rest of the team.

Lionel calls Graf his partner, and the two of them have an understanding that goes beyond commands. As soon as Lionel is dressed in his uniform, Graf knows he is at work.

In January 2015, when Graf was five years old, he played a key role in flushing out two terrorists who were holding a hostage at a printing firm outside of Paris. The terrorists had killed many people who worked for the *Charlie Hebdo* magazine. One of Graf's canine friends, Diesel, a specialist in detecting explosives, had been killed the day before, so the situation was hugely dangerous, but Graf did his job, and in doing so helped to bring calm back to a city that had been gripped by fear. His friend Diesel was awarded the 68th Dickin Medal for the part he played, so he will always be remembered as a hero.

When Graf is not at work, Lionel says they go for long family walks, and Graf is great with the children. He'll probably be retiring soon, and he certainly deserves a long and happy retirement.

Extraordinary Dogs

What makes a dog extraordinary? They all have the same five senses as us—smell, sight, hearing, taste, and touch—but their smell and hearing is far better than ours. Most dogs are smart, loyal, and will protect you if they sense you need protecting. Some can do amazing tricks, but the dogs in this chapter are extraordinary for either behaving in a way that is unusual, or for being exceptional at the jobs they do.

Take this chapter's Hachiko, Capitán, and Masha. These are three dogs whose loyalty and devotion to their owners goes above and beyond what anyone would imagine. They represent three of the most loyal dog breeds—the Akita, the German Shepherd, and the Dachshund. Their owner becomes the most important thing in their lives. Other dogs have plenty of love to share too, such as Jasmine the greyhound, who took it upon herself to nurse rescued animals back to health and happiness.

The other dogs recognized in this chapter are those whose abilities, coupled with their training, mean that they are extraordinary at their jobs. There are the detective dogs, Bear and K9 Killer, who help conservationists look after and rescue animals in danger of extinction or harm. There are the search-and-rescue dogs, Reef and Frida, who have saved many lives and are so good at what they do, they now train other dogs to follow in their pawprints.

Finally, there are a growing number of dogs, like the **KDOG** team, who are helping scientists with such groundbreaking research that they could help thousands of people. There are teams of dogs being trained to detect different types of diseases. At the moment, to test if someone has cancer, doctors have to remove small samples from a person's body, which is then tested. It can be painful and risky, it involves a lot of people, a lot of money, and it can take months. A trained dog can do this in seconds from just a few small cells rubbed onto a cloth. Extraordinary indeed.

Hachiko

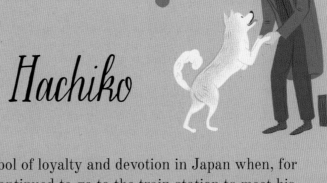

Hachiko became a symbol of loyalty and devotion in Japan when, for almost a decade, he continued to go to the train station to meet his master, even though his master had stopped coming home. He'd suffered a fatal brain haemorrhage at work so never got to say goodbye to his faithful companion.

In early 1924, Professor Ueno, a professor at the faculty of agriculture at the University of Tokyo, brought a little golden Akita puppy home to live with his family in the Shibuya area outside Tokyo. The pair developed a daily routine. Every morning. Professor Ueno and Hachiko would walk to the train station together, and the professor would get on the train to the university. Hachiko would go home and then return to the station at around 3pm to meet his master when he came back. This continued for a year, until one day the professor didn't come home. Even after the professor died, Hachiko continued his 3pm ritual every day for the next 10 years. He never lost hope. His vigil only came to an end in 1935 when Hachiko himself died. Over that time, Hachiko became well known and people would travel to see him and sit with him.

Hachiko's death made national headlines. He was buried alongside his master, and he is remembered every year with a ceremony at the Shibuya train station. In 2009, his story was made into a Hollywood film called *Hachi: A Dog's Tale* starring Richard Gere. Hachiko's devotion mirrors that of Greyfriars Bobby, a Skye Terrier who spent 14 years guarding his owner's grave in Edinburgh in Scotland. Hachiko and Bobby have both been immortalized with bronze statues.

Masha

Little Masha's story is heartbreaking and heartwarming in equal measure. She is a brown Dachshund–Terrier cross who returned to the reception of a hospital in Koltsovo in Russia every day for two years, after her owner was admitted. The pensioner arrived with his pet from a nearby village because he was feeling poorly and couldn't leave Masha behind. He was assessed as Masha waited, but he was kept in and given a bed on a ward. Masha got into a routine of going home when the hospital closed at night and returning again in the morning to see him. She was his only visitor.

Sadly, the man died in December 2013, but Masha continued to turn up at the hospital, every day for a year. Her story hit news websites around the world in November 2014, with the Russian media calling her Russia's very own Hachiko. Her extreme loyalty and big, sorrowful eyes made those who saw her fall in love with her, but Masha wasn't interested in having a new home. The nurses tried—she was adopted three times—but Masha always returned. They hoped that she would eventually find someone she trusted, but in the meantime, they made up a bed for her in the reception, and both hospital workers and visitors brought her food and gave her cuddles. Nurse Alla Vorontsova said, "Masha will always stay here, because she is waiting for her owner. I think that even if we took her to his grave, she would not believe it. She is waiting for him alive, not dead."

In December 2014, the hospital officially adopted her, and she had a permanent bed and all the food and love a dog could want. It was a happy ending for little Masha, and the best Christmas present for the staff and visitors who adored her.

Capitán

When Miguel Guzman brought home a black German Shepherd dog for his 13-year-old son Damian in 2005, they had no idea how extraordinarily loyal and famous he would become. They named him Capitán, but as much as he loved Damain, Capitán adored Miguel.

When Miguel died suddenly a year later, Capitán disappeared from the family home in Villa Carlos Paz in Argentina. The family had no idea where he had gone, but a few days later, they went to visit Miguel's grave, and there was Capitán. He came up to the family barking and howling. The cemetery director, Héctor Bassegas, said he had just turned up there alone, and went around the cemetery until he found Miguel's grave. He hadn't been at the burial, or even to the cemetery before, so how he knew it was his master's grave is a mystery. The following Sunday, the Guzmans returned to the cemetery, and this time Capitán followed them home. He stayed for a while, but went back as it got dark. Every Sunday after that the family would visit the grave and Capitán.

Héctor and the rest of the cemetery staff would feed Capitán and look after him, and he became a permanent fixture there. He would walk around the cemetery during the day, but every evening at 6pm he would lie down by his master's grave and sleep.

Six years into this vigil, Damian said: "I've tried to bring Capitán home several times, but he always comes straight back to the cemetery. I think he's going to be there until he dies too. He's looking after my dad." Damian was right. In 2018, at the grand old age of 15, Capitán did die in that cemetery. His death was not just reported in the town of Villa Carlos Paz, or in nearby Córdoba, Argentina's second-largest city—his story was told around the world. The family scattered his ashes near Miguel's grave—together again at last.

Super Senses

When people and wolves started to live together, both were better off. In return for shelter and warmth, the wolves would sense danger long before it arrived, and detect prey long before their human companions. As wolves were eventually domesticated into dogs, people found other ways of using their amazing senses, and dogs today are trained to help us in so many ways.

A dog's most amazing sense is smell. Even breeds with stubby, squished noses, like the Pug, can smell over 1,000 times better than us. A bloodhound can smell 10 million times better! Bloodhound brothers Tony and Tipper work in Lewa Wildlife Conservancy in Kenya to track a poacher's scent for miles. In experiments, it's been proven that a bloodhound can even track a scent that is two days old.

Dogs can be trained to help people with medical conditions. Miniature poodle Nano is a nut detective. She lives with Yasmine, who has a severe nut allergy. Nano sniffs Yasmine's food and checks her surroundings. If she detects nuts, she paws at the problem. For Yasmine, having Nano around is reassuring, and her red coat alerts others to Yasmine's condition so they take more care. In 2020, other trained dogs helped with the pandemic by detecting scents associated with Covid-19.

Dogs like Jedi are trained to smell changes in their owner's bodies that could be life-threatening. Jedi was trained to alert the parents of diabetic seven-year-old Luke if his blood sugar levels went low. One night, Jedi woke up Luke's parents. Luke's blood-sugar monitor said he was ok, but Jedi didn't give up until they checked on him themselves. Jedi was right—Luke was in danger, but his parents were able to help him, thanks to Jedi!

As well as a superior nose, a dog's hearing is twenty times better than ours. Picking up noises as well as smells enables search-and-rescue dogs like Frida to find people buried under rubble, or lost in the forest, mountains, or snow. Dogs are remarkable, not only in their abilities, but also in their willingness to help us, and in some cases, save our lives.

Reef

Reef is a teacher at the Scuola Italiana Cani Salvataggio, a school for water rescue dogs in Milan, Italy. She is a beautiful black Newfoundland, a breed that is perfectly equipped for a job as a water rescue dog. Newfoundlands have waterproof fur, huge webbed paws, strong jaws, and tremendous strength. They are also calm, fearless, and easy to train. They were bred as working dogs in Newfoundland, Canada, to pull in fishing nets and haul wood from the forest.

The school started as four friends and one dog—another Newfoundland called Mas. They now train hundreds of dogs of all breeds to help lifeguards and coastguards rescue people in the water. It's all about teamwork—dogs and people working together. If the dog gets tired, a person helps. If a person gets tired, the dog helps.

The training can take over a year, and it requires the dogs to jump from boats and helicopters. They are often winched back up after a rescue, so they need the same attributes as Reef—courage and a calm nature. They wear special coats with a handle on the top for both the winch and for people to grab on to.

On average, Reef has saved 20 people a year. He once saved three people on a sailing boat heading for rocks. They threw a rope to Reef and she pulled them out of danger. Now she shows other dogs how it is done. Reef seems to love her job, and is a great teacher. She barks in anticipation when the school director puts on his wetsuit. She knows she's going into the water, and what is expected of her. She is a shining example of her breed, and a superb mentor to the other dogs at the school. Her influence has spread to water rescue teams across Italy and some other European countries. Reef was one of the dogs chosen for an Imax original film, with the fitting title, *Superpower Dogs*.

Jasmine

When British police found Jasmine the greyhound, she was locked in a shed, frightened, mange-ridden, and starving to death. They took her to an animal charity, where she met Geoff Grewcock, director of the Nuneaton and Warwickshire Wildlife Sanctuary. He took her with him to the sanctuary to nurse her back to health.

After her recovery, Jasmine gave back all the care and love she had received from the staff by fostering many orphaned animals that were brought to the sanctuary. Her first foster "child" was Roxy the fox cub, who had been tied to a railing and left to die. She was small and weak, and things didn't look good—until Jasmine decided to look after her. She climbed into Roxy's basket and started to lick her in the same way a mother fox would have done.

To the staff's amazement, Roxy responded, and it was the start of her full recovery. Greyhound and fox became inseparable, and both stayed at the sanctuary together. Following her success with Roxy, Jasmine went on to care for over 100 animals, from rabbits to owls, guinea pigs to badgers. She was a gentle, affectionate, and big-hearted carer to them all.

She had a special relationship with Bramble, a roe deer fawn who was probably abandoned by her mother. She was only a few weeks old when she arrived at the sanctuary, and Jasmine became her mother. She cuddled up with Bramble to keep her warm, and licked her to groom the fawn's fur. Bramble walked between Jasmine's legs, and they kissed each other all the time. Bramble probably thought Jasmine was her mother, until it was time for her to be released into the wild again when she was fully grown. Jasmine died in 2011 at the age of 10, much to the sadness of all those at the sanctuary, human and animal. As their website says, she was truly one of a kind.

Frida

Among all the brave and brilliant search-and-rescue dogs, Frida stands out as truly exceptional. She is a Golden Labrador Retriever who served in the Mexican Navy for nine years, helping to uncover earthquake victims in Haiti, Guatemala, Ecuador, and in her home nation of Mexico. Frida served in 53 missions in all. She first showed how amazing she was after a devastating earthquake in Haiti in the Caribbean in 2010. She helped to find and rescue 12 people who were buried under the rubble of collapsed buildings. In her uniform of protective coat, goggles, and blue boots, Frida went to work, scrambling over rubble, helped by her handlers who held on to her coat to support her as she sniffs to find a scent.

She became a symbol of hope to Mexicans after two large earthquakes there in 2017. One of them devastated parts of the capital, Mexico City, as well as other regions in Central Mexico. Many buildings collapsed, and there were a lot of people unaccounted for and feared dead. Frida and the rest of the Navy's canine sniffer unit spent days searching for them, climbing over rubble and burrowing through holes. They were hailed as heroes, and Frida was their superhero.

When she retired in 2018, the Mexican Navy gave Frida an official retirement ceremony, and it was reported in newspapers around the world. Even the Mexican president at the time, Enrique Peña Nieto, tweeted about her, saying she had saved more than 50 lives. Frida was there when the city of Puebla unveiled a beautiful bronze statue of her, made out of old keys. She is depicted in her goggles, harness, and boots, with her trainer, Israel Arauz, nearby.

Underneath it says: "Memorable symbols of the strength Mexicans can have when we decide to come together for great causes." After retiring, Frida continued to be of service to Mexico and the Navy by helping to guide and train the next generation of search-and-rescue hero dogs.

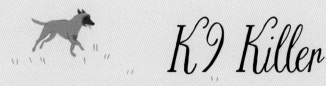

K9 Killer

K9 Killer is a Belgian Malinois, whose name might make you think that he is a scary dog. The only people who need to fear him, however, are poachers and hunters in Kruger National Park in South Africa. He is actually gentle, adventurous, and a real canine hero. K9 Killer works with a team of wildlife rangers and other dogs to stop poachers from killing endangered southern white rhino for their valuable horns. The dogs go through two years of training to get their noses used to the scents of all the wild animals in the park. That way, they can just pick out the human scents among all the others they are exposed to while tracking.

When poachers are spotted in Kruger, handlers and dogs jump into a helicopter and fly to where they were last seen. The dogs set to work as soon as they land, using their finely tuned senses of smell, sight, and hearing to track the poachers. The whole team is brave and brilliant, but K9 Killer has made the biggest contribution, capturing over 115 poachers in his first four years of service. He even saved the life of his handler, Amos Mzimba, when a poacher was shooting at him.

The team at Kruger wrote to the PDSA in 2016 telling them about his achievements, and K9 Killer was awarded the PDSA Gold Medal for his bravery and dedication. He was even rewarded with a visit from royalty when the UK's Prince Harry went to meet him on a trip to Kruger.

The team's work, and that of other teams around the country, has been a conservation success story. According to the Save The Rhino organization, the population of southern white rhinos has increased from a few hundred to 18,000 today. The northern white rhinos haven't fared so well. There are now only two left. The last male died in 2019. This underlines how important the work of these conservation teams are to their survival.

Bear

Bear is a striking Australian Koolie—a high-energy dog with bright blue eyes, alert ears, and a sharp mind. He is one of a growing group of detection dogs that help conservationists to find and protect wildlife. Bear's particular specialty is koalas.

Bear became a national hero in 2019, when devastating bushfires raged through large areas of Australian forest. Many people had to flee the fires. Some lost their homes, and some tragically lost their lives, but even more animals were affected. Most kangaroos and wallabies were able to flee the fires. Birds flew away. Wombats, snakes, and reptiles hid underground, but the slow-moving, tree-dwelling koalas could do nothing to escape. Up to 30 percent of the koala population are thought to have perished in New South Wales, and many more were injured or orphaned.

Bear is specially trained to find koala poop. Where there is poop, there will be a koala in the tree above it. Once Bear had found the koala, animal welfare officers could examine it. They rehomed the healthy ones, treated those with burns, and looked after the babies until they were ready to go back to the wild.

So how did Bear become a koala detective? His first owners rejected him because he was hyperactive and toy obsessed—but these are just the qualities that the trainers of search-and-rescue dogs look for. They adopted Bear from an animal shelter and put him into training straight away. First they got him looking for toys, and then they got him looking for toys that smelled of koala poop. Eventually, Bear was searching for the poop and not the toy. It's all a game to him and he doesn't even realize the important work he is doing. To him, every day, every search is just playing, but to the koalas, he is the difference between life and death. His work has made him famous for the valuable conservation role he played in one of Australia's worst ever disasters.

KDOGs

In 2017, the French dog society, Société Centrale Canine awarded ten "hero dog" trophies. One of them was given to Nykios who was recognized for his skills as a cancer detection dog for the Insitut Curie. Nykios is part of the KDOG project, where specialist dogs are taught to detect breast cancer cells in a person's sweat. The aim is to identify cancers early so they can be treated quickly before they grow and spread.

A study in 2010 determined that cancer cells do have a specific smell. This started the research into whether dogs could detect the scent. In 2016, the Institut Curie wanted to investigate this, so they bought Nykios and his teammate Thor, both Belgian Malinois. They chose them because the breed has a superior sense of smell—millions of times better than a human's. They are also intelligent, task-focused, hardworking, and playful. Nykios and Thor were only 18 months old, but the training started straight away, with them being taught to memorize the scent and then find it.

After the training came the tests, which involved 130 women providing both healthy and cancerous cell samples to a laboratory. Four samples were put into testing devices with funnels, so no other smells could distract the dogs. Nykios and Thor would put their noses into the funnels, and if they detected the scent they would sit down. Amazingly, they had a 100% success rate, taking them less than 30 seconds to detect cancer. The Institut have now added a Springer Spaniel called Milou to the team, to see if he will be as good. In 2019, Looping, another Belgian Malinois, was awarded the same trophy as Nykios. Looping is trained to detect a different type of cancer, also achieving a 100% success rate, compared to the 71% of a machine that does the same job.

These dogs offer exciting new prospects for the detection of cancer without the use of surgery and expensive equipment. Quite simply, they will be lifesavers.

Talented Dogs

Dogs continue to surprise us with their talents on TV and on the internet. There are skateboarding dogs, dancing dogs, singing dogs, and even car-driving dogs! Some dogs just go along for the ride, like YouTube star Sisley. She seems happy doing whatever her daredevil owner does—from jet skiing to scuba diving and skydiving. She is a calm, laid back kind of dog, who takes it all in her stride.

Other dogs are trained to do these things on their own, and despite their many natural abilities, training a dog to ride a bike or walk a tightrope requires hours of repetition, a huge amount of patience, and a lot of treats! Young Alexa Lauenburger from Germany and her eight dogs showed the world what a good trainer can achieve when she performed on TV in Germany, Great Britain, and the United States. She and her father work with the dogs to create entertaining routines that wow audiences. The dogs perform together, which demonstrates how well trained they are. They also do things individually, which showcases their natural talents.

This chapter celebrates the many talented dogs from around the world. There are the movie stars: Rin Tin Tin and Lassie, who achieved worldwide fame and thousands of fans long before the internet had been invented. And there are the sporty stars: TreT the parkour expert, Otto the skateboarder, Ricochet the surfer, and Purin the goalkeeper.

Endal was just as talented as any of these dogs, but he put his talents into helping a man who needed him. He helped him dress, eat, wash, and shop, but more importantly he helped rebuild the man's life.

And one dog is a phenomenon. Chaser knew the names of, and could retrieve, over 1,000 toys. He had the widest vocabulary of any known animal. His owner and trainer wholeheartedly believed you could train a dog to do just about anything.

Pal (Lassie)

Lassie is the most famous fictional screen dog of all time. The first Lassie film, *Lassie Come Home*, was a huge hit in 1943, telling the story of how Lassie made her way home to her family after they were forced to sell her to a rich landowner miles away. Lassie was played by a male Rough Collie called Pal.

Born in 1940, Pal came to live with animal trainer Rudd Weatherwax. His owner asked Weatherwax to cure him of his uncontrolled barking and fondness for chasing motorcycles. Weatherwax cured the barking, but not the motorcycle habit, so the owner gave Pal to Weatherwax in return for the money he owed him. Weatherwax loved Collies, so he was happy to keep Pal. He began training him, and one of the things he taught him to do was to go and find his son at dinnertime. Pal would tug on the son's sleeve to let him know that dinner was ready. That was to prove a useful skill in the Lassie films, which portrayed a special relationship between a boy and his dog.

When the Hollywood studio was casting for the role of Lassie, around 300 dogs auditioned. They gave the job to a beautiful show dog, who was to be trained for the role by Weatherwax. Before the show dog's training was complete, the director decided to shoot a dramatic river scene in California because the conditions were so perfect. The show dog wouldn't enter the water, so Weatherwax suggested that Pal do the scene. It involved swimming the river, hauling himself out, lying down without shaking his coat, crawling on his side and then collapsing, exhausted. Pal did it in one take. Hollywood movie mogul Louis B. Mayer saw the footage and said: "Pal had entered that water, but Lassie had come out."

Pal went on to play the role for the next 11 years in six blockbuster films and two TV pilots. The pilots secured a TV show that ran for almost 20 years, starring Pal's son, Pal Junior, with his old dad watching on from his basket on set.

RIN TIN TIN

Rin Tin Tin

During the last few months of World War I, Corporal Lee Duncan was one of the first to enter the village of Flirey in France after German troops had retreated. He found a kennel in which a frightened German Shepherd was protecting her five puppies. One of those puppies became Rin Tin Tin, a huge movie star of the 1920s.

Duncan returned to his home in the United States with Rin Tin Tin and his sister Nanette. They were named after little wool dolls that French children made as good luck charms, which they sometimes gave to soldiers who liberated their towns and villages.

Duncan began to teach Rin Tin Tin tricks and became obsessed by the idea of him becoming a movie star. The day came when Warner Bros., then a small family studio, agreed to cast Rin Tin Tin as a wolf in a movie. They did have a real wolf playing the role, but he wouldn't do as he was told, so Rin Tin Tin stepped in and his star potential was unleashed. His big break came when he got the starring role in a film in 1923 called *Where the North Begins*. It was a huge success and is credited with rescuing Warner Bros. from going out of business. Today, Warner Bros. is a huge Hollywood studio, producing blockbusters such as the Harry Potter and Batman movies.

Rin Tin Tin starred in 23 films for Warner Bros. and became a well-known movie star. At the height of his fame, he received thousands of fan letters. When he retired, one of his sons took over the role in films, and so continued a long tradition of new Rin Tin Tins, all direct descendants. Rin Tin Tin died at the age of 16. Newspapers and magazines around the world published articles about him but Lee Duncan didn't want a fuss. He buried his pal in his backyard in a quiet ceremony. Later, when he sold the house, he took Rin Tin Tin to France to bury him in his homeland. His grave can be found in the famous pet cemetery just outside Paris.

The Lauenburger Allstars

Alexa Lauenburger has a troop of eight enormously talented dogs—Emma, Jennifer, Katy, Maya, Nala, Sabrina, Sally, and Speck. Together they won *Das Supertalent* (Germany's version of the ... *Got Talent* TV show) in 2017. Alexa was just 10 years old at the time, but it was the start of worldwide fame for them all. Alexa's father is an animal trainer, so Alexa was brought up around dogs, and she watched how her father trained them. It was natural for her to pick up his skills and techniques, and from a young age she was working with the dogs, too. She said she would rush home from school, do her homework, and then go out to see the dogs. She spent as much time as she could with them. At the age of 7 she surprised her father with a dog show for his birthday.

After winning the German show, they went on to star in *Britain's Got Talent* and *America's Got Talent: The Champions*, becoming finalists in both. Alexa is talented, but it is the dogs that are the superstars, entertaining the world with their amazing energy, skills, character, and brilliance. In 2019, Alexa and her father had their sights set on another worldwide achievement—getting a Guinness World Record. They didn't just get one world record, though—they got five!

The first was for the most dogs in a conga line. The dogs were moving in a line in height order, all on their back legs with the front paws on the dog in front. On her own, Emma holds two records: the fastest dog to jump five hurdles on hind legs, and the fastest dog to hop 10 m (32 ft) on hind legs. Jennifer has the record for the fastest 5-m (16-ft) backward walk, and Maya has the record for the most spins by a dog in 30 seconds. Who knows what amazing things Alexa and her beloved dog stars will achieve next?

Canine Film Stars

In 2011, a little Jack Russell called Uggie shot to stardom when he appeared in silent movie The Artist. *His tricks weren't jawdropping, but his talent and his charm won over audiences around the world.*

Uggie received many awards but he never achieved the ultimate—a star on Hollywood's Walk of Fame. Only three dogs have one—Rin Tin Tin, Lassie, and a German Shepherd called Strongheart, who was a war hero before he became the first big movie star in the 1920s. Strongheart appeared in six Hollywood movies, and his performances prompted the German Shepherd to become a popular breed in the United States.

After this, many classic children's movies featured some incredible dog actors. A standout performer was Terry, the Cairn Terrier who appeared in more than 20 movies in the 1930s and 40s, including playing the character of Toto in *The Wizard of Oz.*

Later, filmmakers began to use computer animation to make a dog talk or behave in human ways, just like Fly in the film *Babe.* Nine dogs were trained to be Fly. The filmmakers did have a robotic dog if needed, but the real dogs were so well trained that they performed most of the scenes themselves. The only thing animated was Fly's mouth when she spoke.

In 2019, a Disney film was released about Togo and the incredible rescue mission to Nome in Alaska (see page 21). Togo never got the recognition he deserved in the story, but the younger dog, Balto, was given a statue in Central Park. This film aims to redress that balance, and the dog who played Togo was seven-year-old Diesel, a Siberian husky from Canada, who is actually one of Togo's descendants. Diesel is a trained sled dog, not a trained actor, and the film is as real as the director could make it. Diesel's performance would make his great-great-granddaddy very proud.

TreT

TreT made quite a name for himself online for being as agile as a cat—running up trees, bouncing off walls, and letting few obstacles get in his way. But TreT is not a cat. He is a stocky, fearless Staffordshire Bull Terrier with boundless energy and enthusiasm.

TreT's Ukrainian owner and trainer Eugene Elchaninov turned him into a star in the parkour community. Parkour, which is also called free-running, is an improvised sport, usually with human participants. They make urban landscapes look like jungle gyms, as they run and jump and somersault across rooftops, down staircases, and over walls. Eugene taught TreT to do the same, and as with most Staffordshire Bull Terriers, his strong leg muscles gave him extra bounce. His natural ability enables him to spring from one surface to the next with ease.

His videos have had millions of views, and his athleticism is quite remarkable. He is also a joy to watch, because he clearly loves what he is doing, and he loves the encouragement and applause he gets from the people watching him. He is also faster than most of the humans he is running with. He can balance on posts like a cat, run along the top of walls like a cat, and jump over things almost ten times his height, and still land on all four paws, just like a cat.

There are other parkour canine stars, too. There's Roxy, the Thai Ridgeback from Hawaii, and Neo, the Border Collie from the UK. All three of these dogs display the same physical characteristics as dogs who compete in agility competitions—speed, strength, balance, and finesse. They also share the same mental characteristics—intuition, and the ability to make lightning-fast decisions, changing course in a split second to prevent failure or injury. These dogs clearly love the challenge of running over urban landscapes, or through a specially laid out course at a dog show. Their wagging tails say it all.

Otto

If you were walking in a beautiful coastal park in Lima, Peru, in 2015, you might have seen something you didn't quite believe—a 12-kg (27-lb) English Bulldog skateboarding his way into the world record books. His name was Otto, but skateboarding was not his only talent.

His owners Luciana Viale and Robert Rickards had seen footage of Tillman, another bulldog whose skills on a board were impressive. They decided to introduce Otto to the joys of skateboarding when he was a puppy. After a spell of chewing the wheels, Otto realised it was more fun to ride. English Bulldogs are often very relaxed, but Otto was as energetic and athletic as his owners. They took him to the beach often, where he learned to surf and skim-board, but skateboarding was Otto's special skill.

Otto was three years old when he attempted the Guinness World Record for the longest skate under a human tunnel. It was quite a spectacle with 30 people lined up along a path in Parque de Miraflores, overlooking the Pacific Ocean. And Otto didn't put a paw wrong. He pushed the board with his front leg and hopped on top of it as it went downhill. He steered the board through the tunnel, continuing to propel himself to the end. His tongue was dangling from his wide mouth, and it looked as if he was smiling from ear to ear. He'd done it, and was officially awarded the record then and there. After that he starred in a TV advert and was nominated for a World Dog Award in the "Hot Dog" category. He was beaten by Dally, the horse-riding dog.

Otto sadly died at the end of 2019, but not before becoming a daddy to four gorgeous bulldog pups, after Luciana and Robert found him a girlfriend, Lolita. There are still a few skateboards around the house, so maybe one of them will follow in their father's pawprints.

Purin

Beagles were bred as hunting dogs to track rabbits and foxes, so their top skill is usually their sense of smell. They are known to be friendly, smart and excitable, but not at all easy to train, except for Purin. She is no ordinary Beagle.

Purin has learned so many tricks that she has three world records to her name, one of them for something you wouldn't imagine a dog could do. To say she has a world record in catching balls wouldn't amaze anyone—all dogs can catch balls, can't they? What is different about Purin, is that she doesn't catch them with her mouth—she catches them in her paws, like a goalkeeper. She sits on her hind legs, with her paws raised in anticipation, and she grabs the ball at just the right time. She's fast, too! She broke her own Guinness World record in 2015 by catching 14 balls in under a minute.

Her owner, Makoto Kumagai, has also taught Purin to skip with him, walk on her hind legs, do pawstands and walk on her front paws, skateboard, and balance on a fitness ball like a circus performer. She does all of these things effortlessly, and has since added two more world records to her collection—one with Kumagai for the most skips by a dog and a person in one minute, and the other for the fastest 10 m (33 ft) walking on a ball.

According to her owner, Purin can do over 100 tricks, and her videos online have millions of views. She is a delight to watch, often sporting little vests and sometimes boots. Her talents are quite staggering, and she seems to love everything she does.

Some of the credit must go to Kumagai, who has managed to train the type of dog that most people find too hard, but Purin is a natural, and an exception to her breed. She is now an old lady, but she is still playing ball and skateboarding around Japan with Kumagai.

Ricochet
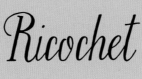

A dog on a surfboard is not something you see on many of the world's beaches, but in California, on the west coast of the United States, it is not unusual. There is a whole series of summer competitions for surfing dogs, but there is one dog who has taken her talents to another level. She is a beautiful Golden Retriever named Ricochet.

Born in 2008, she was raised as an assistance dog to help people with disabilities. Ricochet showed real potential, opening doors and closets, switching on lights, fetching, and carrying, but then she discovered the fun of chasing birds. No matter how hard her owner and trainer Judy Fridono tried, she couldn't get Ricochet out of the habit. She was just too energetic and playful to be an assistance dog.

Instead of giving up on Ricochet, Judy focused on what Ricochet was good at—balancing on a body board in a paddling pool. Surfing came naturally to Ricochet after that, and she took part in her first competition when she was only 18 months old. As if that wasn't impressive enough, Ricochet did something that catapulted her into a different league. In 2009, she was asked to surf with Patrick Ivison, a quadriplegic teenager. The idea was for Ricochet to surf alongside him, but at the end of the wave, Ricochet jumped off her board and onto his. Ricochet was the perfect counterbalance, ensuring that the board didn't topple over, and if it did, Patrick could hold on to Ricochet while she swam.

After that initial ride, they held a fundraiser that raised thousands of dollars for Patrick's physical therapy. From that moment on, Judy realized that Ricochet could serve people with disabilities in a different way, and now she is a unique therapy dog. She brings joy to both children and adults alike in a way that no person could. She is a very special dog, who delights in helping others and in turn changes their lives for the better.

Chaser

Chaser was a canine brainiac who had the largest known vocabulary of any non-human. She was a Border Collie, a dog bred for its intelligence and ability to understand commands—whistles, words, and gestures—so they could help farmers to round up livestock. Chaser had that in her DNA, but instead of teaching Chaser to round up sheep, her owner John Pilley, turned her into one of the smartest dogs ever known.

Her education started when she was just a two-month-old puppy. Dr. Pilley, a retired psychology professor, brought a blue ball home and rolled it to her. "Chaser," he said, "this is Blue." And so the ball became Blue. A stuffed horse was Bamboozle. A squeaky train was Choo Choo. And so it went on, until Chaser knew the name of, and could retrieve, 1,000 toys. Dr. Pilley and his wife had to label each one or they would forget its name. Chaser rarely forgot.

Chaser understood that "ball" was a word that meant a group of objects, so she could bring Blue or any of her other balls. She also figured out what new words meant. If she was asked to find a new toy among her familiar toys, she would deduce that she wasn't being asked to fetch something she knew, so it had to be the thing she didn't know. She knew other commands too, such as "Nose Frisbee," which meant touch Frisbee with her nose, and "Take Blue to Frisbee." Dr. Pilley's work with Chaser led to a new understanding of dogs' intelligence. He wrote a book about her in 2013, and told *The New York Times*: "The big lesson is to recognize that dogs are smarter than we think, and given time, patience, and enough enjoyable reinforcement, we can teach them just about anything."

Dr. Pilley died in 2018, aged 89. Chaser died a year later, aged 15, which is 105 in human years. A bronze statue of her has been commissioned in her hometown of Spartanburg in South Carolina, with Dr. Pilley's footprints by her side.

Endal

Endal was a Golden Labrador named "Dog of the Millennium" by *Dogs Today* magazine. He was a PDSA Gold Medal winner, because of his devotion to his owner, and Endal also became an ambassador for service dogs everywhere. Endal's story is Allen Parton's story too. Allen is a Royal Navy veteran who had suffered serious head injuries in the Gulf War in 1991. When he woke up in hospital, his body was shattered and no one could understand what he was saying. He couldn't even recognize his wife and children. Allen became deeply depressed, until he met Endal in 1998. Endal was a trainee assistance dog whose efforts had been half-hearted until he met Allen. Suddenly, he was enthusiastic and full of purpose. It was as if he knew how sad and broken Allen was, and he really wanted to help.

Endal began to learn what Allen needed through signs—a touch of the cheek meant to get the razor, a touch on the head meant hat. Eventually the desire to communicate with his dog meant that Allen began to form words, and his speech returned slowly. Endal helped Allen do everything, from getting his wheelchair, his breakfast, his shopping, and his clothes, to helping him get money out of the cashpoint (or ATM). They became well known locally, then international film crews wanted to see this incredible "cashpoint dog."

When Allen was knocked out of his wheelchair by a car, and lay unconscious in a car park. Endal dragged Allen into the recovery position, pulled the wheelchair blanket over him, pushed Allen's phone into his hand, and then ran into a hotel to get help. Allen was fine, and Endal was a hero. Endal's last job before he died in 2009 was to teach his son EJ (Endal Junior) how to care for Allen's needs. Allen said his remarkable friend was "living proof that angels don't just come on two legs." Allen has now set up a charity, Hounds for Heroes, enabling more injured veterans to experience the life-changing power of man's best friend.

Caring for Dogs and Puppies

Puppies are adorable bundles of fur and fun, but they need lots of attention and care. Putting in time and training in the early months means your puppy should grow up to be a happy and well-behaved dog.

Make your puppy feel safe
Young puppies need lots of comfort when you bring them home. They are away from their mothers for the first time, so they need cuddles and a warm place to go to when they need to sleep – a crate or soft bed with a blanket and furry toy is ideal.

Plenty of play
When they are awake, puppies love to play and explore. As they get older, they love to chew. Play games with them and give them toys so they don't chew your best shoes or furniture. Learning what they like to play with (and eat) will be useful when it comes to training them.

Hello world
When your puppy has been vaccinated, you can take them out to meet other dogs and people. Carry them at first because the outside world will be scary. Get them used to a lead and collar or harness straight away.

Training

The most important thing about training a dog is to be consistent so they understand what is expected of them. Decide as a family how you are going to train your puppy —the words you are going to use, how you will reward your puppy for doing things you would like, and what you will do when they misbehave. Don't scold them if they have an accident. Just take them outside, and give them plenty of praise and a treat when they get it right.

Food

Changing your puppy's food suddenly is not a good idea. Stick with what they are used to and change their food gradually to avoid them getting an upset tummy.

Grooming

It's a good idea to get puppies used to a brush in the early months. They might want to bite it, but they need to feel comfortable with you grooming and touching different parts of their bodies.

Leave them alone

When your puppy is settled and happy, start to leave them alone for short periods. They may whine, but they need to get used to not being around you all the time. Go back to them if they get distressed. Build up the time you are away from them gradually.

Exercise

As well as play, sleep, and food, dogs need exercise. Get into a routine, such as a walk after breakfast and then home for a sleep. Most dogs like two walks a day, but it depends on the breed. A high-energy dog like a Collie needs a lot of exercise, but a docile Dachshund will probably be happy with a stroll.

Puppy classes

Many puppies and owners benefit from going to classes for some basic training. Ask your vet if you need some help finding a good class. Doing all this and spending time with your puppy in the early months will lead to a long and happy friendship. Enjoy!

Further Reading

Find out more about the dogs in this book:

Arthur by Mikael Lindnord
Read about Arthur and Mikael's incredible and heart-warming story, from the Columbian jungle to the family home in Sweden.

Bothie the Polar Dog by Ranulph and Virginia Fiennes
Read about Bothie's antics on the Fiennes' awe-inspiring and ambitious expedition.

Chaser by John W. Pilley
This is the joyful story of Professor Pilley and his super-smart dog Chaser, and their daily play regime that turned Chaser into a phenomenon.

Endal by Allen and Sandra Parton
A first-hand account of how Endal the remarkable Labrador puppy came into Allen's life and slowly helped him heal and pull his family back together.

Finding Gobi by Dion Leonard
Finding Gobi during an ultra-marathon across the Gobi Desert is only the beginning of this feel-good adventure story.

War Dog by Damien Lewis
The story of the amazing bond between Polish airman Robert Bozdech and Antis, the puppy he rescued from no-man's land during World War II.

www.guinnessworldrecords.com
Watch the amazing talents of Purin, Otto and Alexa Lauenburger's Allstars.

https://kdog.institut-curie.org
Meet the KDOG team of detective dogs sniffing out cancer.

www.pdsa.org.uk
The official website of the PDSA, where you can see the video award of the award given to K9 Killer by Ricky Gervais.

www.surfdogricochet.com
The website of the remarkable Ricochet, the amazing surfing dog.

www.usc.edu.au
Find out more about Bear and the other detection dogs that support animal welfare.

Acknowledgments

With thanks to: BBC • Huffington Post • Warner Bros • Smithsonian Institution • *Time Magazine* • *The Siberian Times* • Euronews • *Daily Mail* • abc news • The Oregon Encyclopedia • KOIN 6TV • *The Independent* • *The Guardian* • Montrose Heritage Trust • myrepublica.nagariknetwork.com • www.gouvernement.fr • www.australiangeographic.com.au